ASTHMA

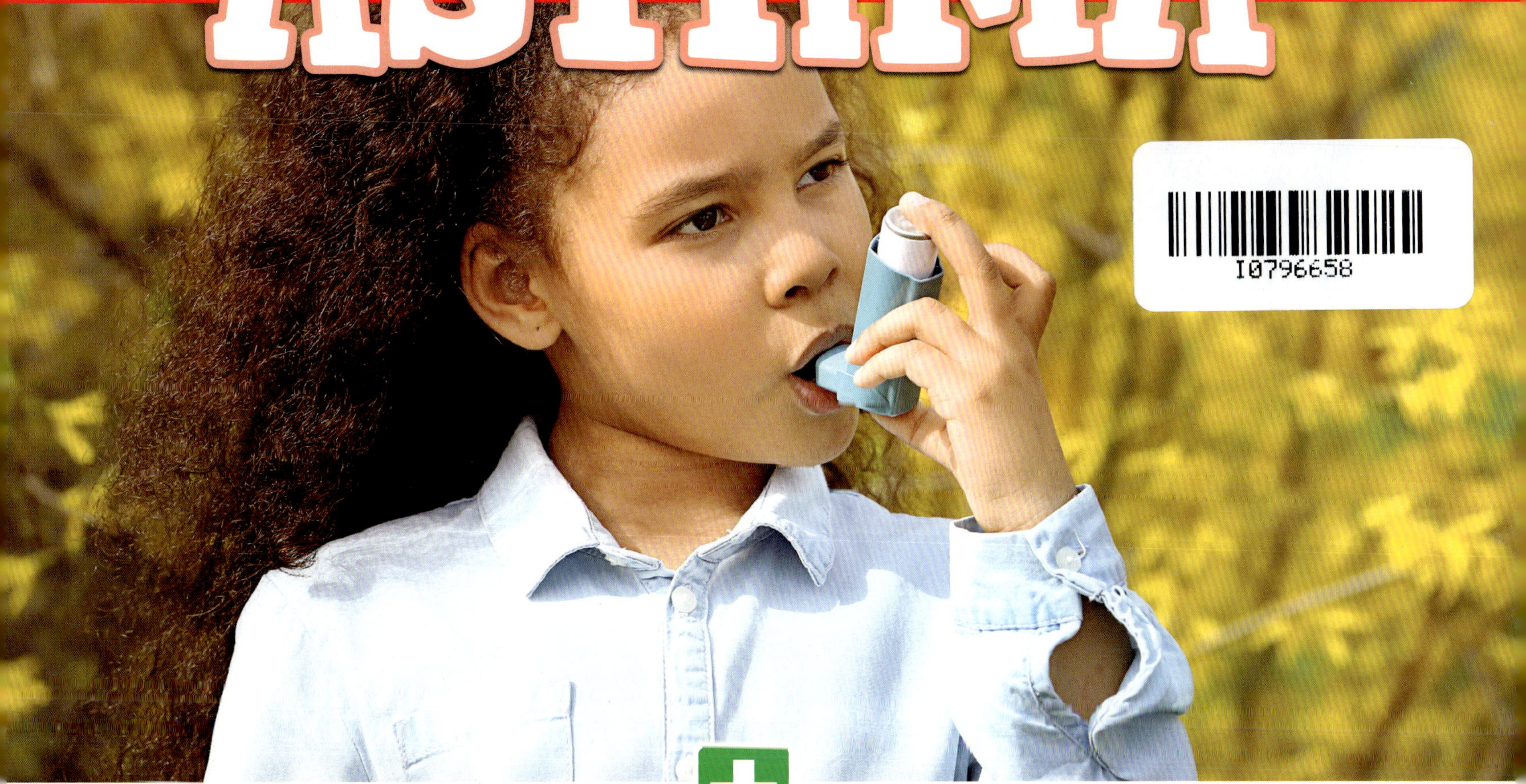

IN CASE OF EMERGENCY

Ryan Smith

www.av2books.com

Step 1
Go to **www.av2books.com**

Step 2
Enter this unique code
AOFHUMN86

Step 3
Explore your interactive eBook!

IN CASE OF EMERGENCY
ASTHMA
Start!

AV2 is optimized for use on any device

Your interactive eBook comes with...

Audio
Listen to the entire book read aloud

Videos
Watch informative video clips

Weblinks
Gain additional information for research

Try This!
Complete activities and hands-on experiments

Key Words
Study vocabulary, and complete a matching word activity

Quizzes
Test your knowledge

Slideshows
View images and captions

View new titles and product videos at www.av2books.com

IN CASE OF EMERGENCY

ASTHMA

Contents

Some people have asthma. Asthma can make it hard to breathe.

An asthma attack can be caused by allergies or too much exercise.

In the United States,
1 out of every 13
people has asthma.

Signs and Symptoms

An asthma attack causes the chest to feel tight.

It also makes a person wheeze or cough.

Stay Calm

It is important to stay calm when someone is having an asthma attack.

Panicking will only make things worse.

Call 9-1-1

Call 9-1-1 if an asthma attack is really bad.

The 9-1-1 operator will need to know your name, where you are, and what the emergency is.

Sit Down

Someone having an asthma attack should sit down.

The person should sit straight so it is easier to breathe.

Use an Inhaler

A person with asthma might have an inhaler. An inhaler gives medicine that helps make breathing easier.

Someone having an asthma attack may need help using his or her inhaler.

Breathe Slow

Taking slow and steady breaths helps a person through an asthma attack.

It is best to breathe in through the nose and out through puckered lips.

Help Arrives

The 9-1-1 operator may send paramedics in an ambulance.

The paramedics might give oxygen from a tank and take the person to the hospital.

PARAMEDIC

Preventative Measures

People with asthma should be careful when running or playing games.

They should also avoid breathing in smoke or other things that could trigger an attack.

More than **3 million** U.S. children had an **asthma attack** in **2020**.

EMERGENCY PROCEDURES

These pages provide detailed information that expands on the emergency found in the book. They are intended to be used by adults as a learning support to help young readers understand the correct responses to each emergency featured in the *In Case of Emergency* series.

Pages 4–5

Some people have asthma. Asthma is a disorder that causes a person's airway to narrow, making breathing difficult. Its severity and triggers vary from person to person. Asthma can be triggered by allergens such as pollen, irritants such as smoke, or increased heart and breath rate from overexertion. There is no cure for asthma, but its symptoms can be managed.

Pages 6–7

An asthma attack causes the chest to feel tight. Symptoms of an asthma attack include a tightening of the chest, trouble breathing or shortness of breath, coughing, and wheezing. People suffering from asthma attacks may also become anxious or panic as they struggle to breathe.

Pages 8–9

It is important to stay calm when someone is having an asthma attack. It is especially important for the person experiencing the asthma attack to stay calm. Should the person start to panic, his or her breaths may become shorter. The airway may tighten and close further. The person assisting someone having an attack should stay calm. This will keep mistakes from being made and will help the person having the attack to stay calm.

Pages 10–11

Call 9-1-1 if an asthma attack is really bad. A call to 9-1-1 should only be placed in emergency situations. Not all asthma attacks are severe enough to warrant calling 9-1-1. Only call 9-1-1 if a person having an asthma attack shows no sign of getting better after taking asthma medication, or if shortness of breath or wheezing symptoms are rapidly becoming worse. In less severe cases, an asthma attack can be treated without the assistance of emergency medical services (EMS) or a doctor.

Pages 12–13

Someone having an asthma attack should sit down. The first step to treat an asthma attack is to remove the victim from the situation causing the attack. This could mean stopping a physical activity or moving away from an irritant that is triggering the attack. The person having the attack should sit in a comfortable position that opens the chest and airway.

Pages 14–15

A person with asthma might have an inhaler. Help the person having the attack use his or her rescue inhaler or other type of medication for asthma. The person having the attack should also loosen any tight-fitting clothing around the chest and neck in order to help open the airway.

Pages 16–17

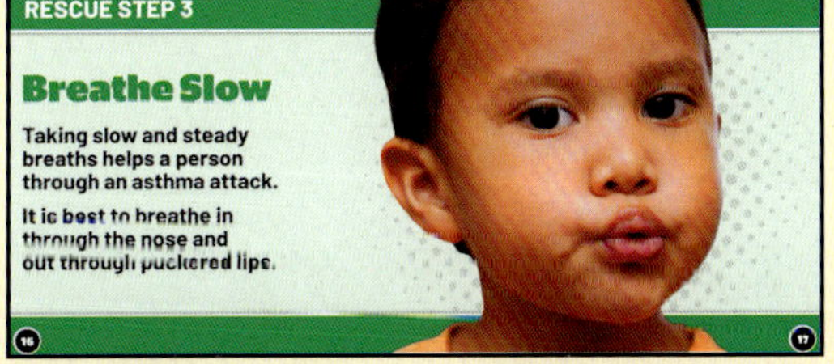

Taking slow and steady breaths helps a person through an asthma attack. An asthma attack makes it difficult to breathe out. A person having an attack should take slow, controlled breaths in through the nose and slow, controlled breaths out through pursed or puckered lips. This will help the person having the attack focus on moving air in and out of the lungs.

Pages 18–19

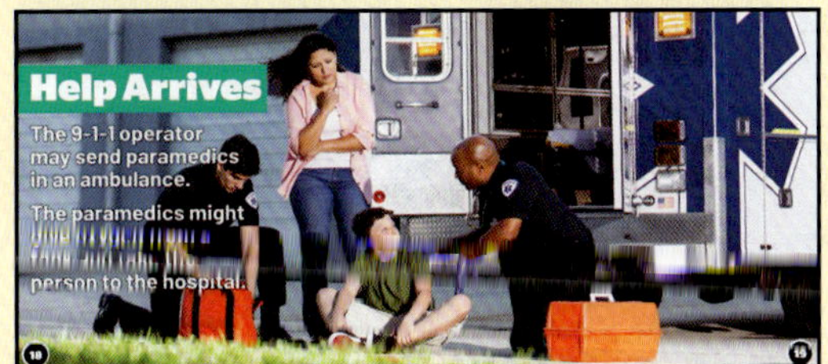

The 9-1-1 operator may send paramedics in an ambulance. If paramedics have been sent, they will assess the situation and monitor the breathing of the person having the asthma attack. Paramedics are trained to provide oxygen from a tank to a person having an attack. They are also trained to administer medicines that will help relax the person's airway and make breathing easier. Even if the attack seems to be over, paramedics may still take the person to a hospital so he or she can be monitored and evaluated by a doctor.

Pages 20–21

People with asthma should be careful when running or playing games. Since there is no cure for asthma, it is up to a person to monitor and treat his or her own symptoms. Doctors may prescribe a long-term medication that is taken daily or a rescue medication to be used when an attack is coming on. A person with asthma must try to avoid situations, activities, or irritants that may trigger an attack. A healthy diet and exercise can strengthen the heart and lungs, which may help make symptoms less severe.

KEY WORDS

Research has shown that as much as 65 percent of all written material published in English is made up of 300 words. These 300 words cannot be taught using pictures or learned by sounding them out. They must be recognized by sight. This book contains 63 common sight words to help young readers improve their reading fluency and comprehension. This book also teaches young readers several important content words, such as proper nouns. These words are paired with pictures to aid in learning and improve understanding.

Page	Sight Words First Appearance
4	an, be, by, can, hard, have, make, much, or, people, some, the, to, too
5	every, has, of, out, states
6	a, also, and
8	important, is, only, things, when, will
10	are, call, if, know, name, need, really, what, where, you, your
12	down, should, so
14	gives, help, her, his, may, might, that, use
16	in, through
18	from, might, take
20	could, other, that, they
21	children, had, more, than

Page	Content Words First Appearance
4	allergies, asthma, asthma attack, emergency, exercise
5	United States
6	chest, person, signs, symptoms
10	operator
12	step
14	inhaler, medicine
16	breaths, lips, nose
18	ambulance, hospital, oxygen, paramedics, tank
20	games, preventative measures, smoke

Published by AV2
14 Penn Plaza 9th Floor New York, NY 10122
Website: www.av2books.com

Library of Congress Cataloging-in-Publication Data

Names: Smith, Ryan, author.
Title: Asthma / Ryan Smith.
Description: New York, NY : AV2, [2021] | Series: In case of emergency | Audience: Ages 5-9 | Audience: Grades 2-3
Identifiers: LCCN 2020014391 (print) | LCCN 2020014392 (ebook) | ISBN 9781791126605 (library binding) | ISBN 9781791126612 (paperback) | ISBN 9781791126629 | ISBN 9781791126636
Subjects: LCSH: Asthma--Juvenile literature. | Medical emergencies--Juvenile literature.
Classification: LCC RC591 .S64 2021 (print) | LCC RC591 (ebook) | DDC 616.2/38--dc23
LC record available at https://lccn.loc.gov/2020014391
LC ebook record available at https://lccn.loc.gov/2020014392

Printed in Guangzhou, China
1 2 3 4 5 6 7 8 9 0 24 23 22 21 20

052020
100919

Project Coordinator: Ryan Smith
Art Director: Terry Paulhus

The publisher acknowledges Alamy, Getty images, iStock, and Shutterstock as its primary image suppliers for this title.